I love you...

Still...

FinDing EsCapes

Achieve, Inspire, Empower.

Finding Escapes
PO Box 15162
New Orleans, LA 70175
Jperry@findingescapes.org

Quantity sales. Special discounts are available on
quantity purchases by corporations, associations,
and others. For details, contact the publisher at
the address above.

ISBN 978-1-7331431-4-1
Printed in the United States of America

FALLING
ROSE PETALS

A Collection of Poems, Memoirs & Reflections

Written By: John H. Perry III

This Book Is Dedicated to My Sons, John IV &
Jonah

"Dreams stay alive only as long as you feed them."

-Unknown

Table of Contents

Table of Contents

Table of Contents

An Open Letter: From Me to You

13 Love Lost Rd.
Broken Heart, LA
Falling Rose Petals-0313

December 13, 2006
Dear _____,

If you think this is about you, chances are it is probably not. Well then again, maybe it is about you. Who cares? Do you? It was thirteen years ago. Right!?

Sincerely Yours,

John Perry III

John Perry III

Introduction: Thirteen Years Later

Being different while growing up was something I tried to deny. The environment I lived in was the same as any inner-city neighborhood. However, living in it was torment. While attending college, I wrestled with frustration and short tempers. I was never the worst kid on the block. I was not anywhere close.

I was a product of my environment. It was hard to adapt not to be around it. Crazy as it sounds, I was used to the mayhem. At that time, I realized people return to past habits. Innately when you fall, you tumble into your comfort zone. It is an easy way out. Typically, we shy away from stepping into different circumstances. People are commonly resistant to change. I was a kid that attended good schools but lived on a battlefield.

It was pressing to sit in a classroom when people you love are on drugs. It makes things gloomier in a place of dysfunction. Discomfort made me feel cursed. The city possesses a thrill. It is a level of excitement that draws you near the negativity. As you read, you can hear the clashes and the cries of change. While being looked at as a success story by family, I felt unsuccessful in things. Trapped by the fear of falling short of what I should become.

Some of the things I penned inside I sincerely do not remember. My first time reading some memoirs was when I converted them into this book. Included are the original poems for you to see. The memoirs shift from sadness, love, and hope.

My teachers initially thought of me as dumb. My speech impediment caused anger; it was

Introduction: Thirteen Years Later

something that haunted me. I would raise my hand to answer a question and hear people laughing as I spoke. Life at this point consisted of many ebbs and flows. The idea of believing your incompetent, illiterate, and wasteful is harsh.

I attended a supplemental academic program. The program was for students that needed reading support. While I read more, my words became clear. Things changed for me after that. When it was time for me to enter middle school, teachers begged my mother to send me to a charter school. She listened and enrolled me at a school on the opposite side of town.

It was my first time being around so many white people. I thought they all were wealthy and smarter than me. Thoughts were fixated in my head subconsciously. The work was rigorous, and the teachers were different. My mother instructed me to work harder. The adversity I faced did the opposite it broke me down.

I struggled more. The gifted English teacher recommended me to another "type" of class. She said this just was not for me. My emotions made me feel abandoned. My body was full of frustrations to the tipping point. All of that changed one day when the class had a poetry lesson. Even with no computer at home, I would get to school early to write. Fury started to subside. My first love was evident. I continued to write poems all year, but when the year was over, so was my writing. Almost seven years would pass until I would write again. During my freshman year

Introduction: Thirteen Years Later

in college, I fell in love. This feeling was undeniable. If you are reading this (yes, I am talking to you), you know my passion. This story is no different from most, but I decided to write my journey down in real-time.

My sentiments of love were ridiculous early on. I surprisingly fell for three girls, including a friend that I blurred the lines. Our friendship remained damaged for years. Eventually, we both matured and talked things over. Another young lady I met seemed to have the foundational pillars I always wanted. The individual made me feel like nothing. Externally my confidence bloomed but hurt inside made me think I was not good enough. Along the way, I was so invested in them. I even broke a heart or two.

I feel horrible for how I treated someone who genuinely loved me. The beautiful woman did not deserve that burden I gave. It was all about me, so I did not care at the time. Those months were a rollercoaster of all sorts. I had dreams of what-if with a girl that I knew was compatible. However, she left just as quickly as she came. She left my soul to bleed. My voice was not strong enough to speak my thoughts.

I was in love with a young lady for over a decade. I struggled to let go of her. People grow and change, but I attempted to hold on to something that had passed. All of this withheld me psychologically. I am robust enough to say it now. I was not the man I should have been to my former significant other. It was because I cared for someone else. These things caused adultery, lack of empathy, picking

Introduction: Thirteen Years Later

pointless arguments, and overall turmoil. I felt trapped to know she was not the one for me. My sincere apologies. Since healing, I have prospered with my dreams. I have become a happier individual; it is weird how life works. I know whatever is in store for me next will be extraordinary. The past has passed and will not happen again. You see, I was a kid that could not express my heart, so I placed it on paper.

The process is allowing you into my heart, brain, and spirit. This ink is my blood bleeding on the pages of this book. The memories of the past can dictate the future in our current present. To let go, we must allow things to leave. This book is my release.

Here is the truth of my thoughts that I wrote. I kept the texts inside my closet. Ironically, the writings were in a box. Now I am not only coming out of the box, but I am letting it all out. Most importantly, I am fulfilling a goal. The material is not the best (nor do I care for it to be). It is what I felt at the time. As a result, I have made limited edits. It is all there as it was almost fifteen years ago. I appreciate you for taking the time to read this. Even if this is the only one you read.

-JP3

My First Expressions

1

What I Feel for You

The way I feel for you cannot be described in
words
Only described in the actions I display towards you
The characteristics of you
Have changed my character as a man
For the better that is of course
What has taken course
I could have never thought of
Nowadays, I cannot help but to blush
Any time your name is brought up

You know whats funny kid
This entire situation is
I would be lying
If I told you I've never thought of you time to time
Thinking of what it would be like
With you inside of my hands
Just As a Clock
And Like that I watch
With every passing tick
With every passing second
Hoping for the best
Praying that you open your eyes and see
What I've already discovered in you
The rhythm that I move to comes from the beat
The beat of my heart
That you have the power to control
But be gentle Is All I ask
Treat me with the tenderness and affection
That I've displayed towards you
Don't ask too many question
For the simple reason that
I can be all of the answers
I'm not the smartest person
But I know I would be stupid to let you pass
At Times It Becomes Hard to Concentrate

Expressing Feelings

I would be lying

If I told you I had never thought of you time to time

Thinking of what it would be like

With you inside of my hands

Just like a clock, and like that I watch

With every passing tick, with every passing second

Hoping for the best

Praying that you open your eyes and see

What I have already discovered in you

The rhythm that I move to comes from the beat of
my heart

That you have the power to control

Be gentle is all I ask

Treat me with the tenderness and affection

That I have exhibited towards you

Do not ask too many questions

I can be all the answers

At times it becomes hard to concentrate

My feelings have been cemented

They are concrete for you

Many different faces I have seen

Expressing Feelings

But the past is over
All I know now is you
Because truthfully, it is all that matters
There is no need to ask how you feel
I have already taken notice
The way you look at me
The way that you smile at me
The way that you hold me
The way that your body tightens next to me
Will you follow our path of love?
My heart is waiting for you in the future
Take the path to meet me there
But do not be late
Life is short

My Heart is Heavy

I cannot stand here and deny my smile

At the same time my insides are stained from the
dried tears of my eye

Honestly, there is no limit for where I want us to be

I am afraid of getting hurt again

Me sad you cannot see...

I apologize sincerely, but I dearly feel distraught

I have learned countless lessons in life, but this is
one I do not want to be taught

It is a direct strike to my pride, but this needs to
be said

What is understood usually needs not to be
explained

Still though I will try to explain

The thoughts of my mind frame

I will try to show you

Why I am

What I am

I will try to show you

Why I did

What I did

Then acted

The way I acted

And later my reaction to what happened

My Heart is Heavy

What was I thinking?

Traveling so far into the dim light

I am a man

I messed up

I admit that

It was my mistake and whatever your decision may
be

I will learn to live with that

It was my fault

I hope you understand

If you do not

I will live with that

Even if it hurts tenfold on my body

Hopefully though you will unbreak my flower of a
heart

Then it will blossom, and my tears will be washed
away in the waves

And I will live with that instead

The Roses

Your love is as bold as a red rose

My shyness is as blue as a violet

Your taste is as sweet as Chocolate

Your love is my warmth

You are a beautiful dove

Towering in the skies above

The tender words from you lips

Play sweet harp music to my heart

Your sweet kisses are like a warm summer's honey

From the beginning of the start

Your different differences took a toll on my heart

I knew from that moment that I had to learn your name

Just as that

Is what I received (say your name)

True Words

True words being said

At times I cannot believe myself

I cannot even imagine how I received the
opportunity

To converse with a lovely person such as yourself

Caught up within the whirlwind

It got taken for granted

With my words being kept inside because of fear of
what may happen

My hesitation to tell you my true feelings

Have left me in a lonely place saddened

The situation at hand has taught me something

That is to never let something so precious slip
away

Especially if it means as much to you as you mean
to me

Day 1

There is no denying what I feel for you

It is no mystery this whole time I have been real
with you

It is no secret I am happy to be with you

I will cross 1 million mountains, and swim 1000
rivers

Just so I can see you

I may have been blind before, but now all I am
seeing is you

No doubt about it, there is no me without you

The future holds me holding you

Wiping your tears of joy

Caressing your body

Consoling you

The second happiest day of my life was when I met
you

The first will be when you say I do

You Ask Me

Y ou ask me...

Why do I smile?

That is easy...

Because I am happy to be with you

You tell me...

My eyes are beautiful

That is easy...

You see I have been looking at you

You ask me...

Why is my skin so smooth?

That is easy...

My fingers have massaged you

You ask me...

Why is my heart so tender?

That is easy...

That is the benefit of loving you

You ask me...

Why am I so quiet?

That is easy...

You see I have been thinking of you

You ask me...

Why am I so sweet?

That is easy...

You Ask Me

Your lips arc honey to me

You ask me...

Why am I never down?

That is easy...

I have something too beautiful to be sad

You ask me...

How do I understand?

That is easy...

You are the motivation behind this man

You ask me...

Am I too good to be true?

That is easy...

Everything that I do, reflects you

tell

You ask me
That am I always quiet
That's easy
you see I've been thinking of you
you tell me
Why I'm so sweet
That's easy
your lips are like honey to me
you ask me
Why Am I never mad
That's easy
I have something too beautiful to be sad
you tell me
your happy I understand
That's easy
you are the motivation behind this Man
you tell me
That I'm too good to be true
That's easy
you see everything that I do is a reflection of you

Nothing that've Ever seen in life compares to you
Nothing as beautiful, Nothing as sensitive, Nothing as true
Nothing as sweet, Nothing as caring, Nothing as intelligent as you
Me minus you equals nothing
And nothing in life compares to that
The aspect of you would add something to my emptiness
And nothing in my wildest thoughts could of thought of
that
I confess I have been strucken by Eros bow in my breast
The way that I feel for you
Nothing compares to that

Nothing in Life

Nothing that I have ever seen in life compares to
you

Nothing as beautiful

Nothing as sensitive

Nothing as true

Nothing as sweet

Nothing as caring

Nothing as intelligent as you

Me minus you equals nothing, and nothing in life
compares to that

A portion of you would add something to my
emptiness

Nothing in my wildest thoughts, could have
thought of that

I confess I have been stricken by Eros's arrow in
my breast

The way I feel for you

Nothing in life compares to that

Every second I have with you, I am thankful for
that

What has happened to me?

I imagined I would never experience that

My past road is far behind, but I have been hurt
before

I swore I never wanted to travel the path of love
anymore

Nothing in Life

But I laid eyes upon your canvas, the picture
painted was so beautiful to my pupils

And nothing in life is as fulfilling as that

Nor as appreciated as I appreciate what has
occurred

Two ever distant nebulas to meet in the stars

With you by my side you can create

A product within my mathematical equation

And nothing will grow into something with you

Ever Since

Ever since the first day I met you

The effect of you on me has been influential

I knew you were different than the rest

Maybe it was the way the light illuminated on you

And the way it did not on the rest

Maybe it was the glossy sparkle of your eye

Whatever it may have been

It caught my attention as well as my heart

Every moment I have spent with you has been
cherished

At first, I did not realize what I had

Until, I opened my eyes to see what I had

At that very moment

I knew you were the one

In My Lifetime

I have seen many faces

From the peaks of the Rockies

To the islands of the Pacific

From the valleys of Egypt

To the pearls of Persia

All in my lifetime...

I have seen the secrets of the Olmec

The traditions of the natives

The exotics of the tropics

The rivers of the everglades

All in my lifetime...

From the great wall of the Zhou

To the samurai of Japan

From the winter of Russia

To the temples of Buddha

All in my lifetime...

Every wind from north to south

Every breeze from east to west

But nothing compares to being in love with you

In this lifetime...

Pain

P_{ain...}

The way I feel inside is indescribable

I cannot consume the pain

It shows in my face

It is undisguisable

Betrayed

Love is rotten

The end is bitter

This twisted sour tasting world

I trust only a select few

Because others are not true

No secrets

No lies

Everything in the open

With nothing to hide

It hurts badly

Pain...

My mind tells me it will be over in the morning

Soon as the sun sets as with the passing day

Pain...

It lingers

I still feel betrayed

By a friend

Pondering Life

2

Sadness and Joy

The sadness of my joy

Has me here contemplating what I have been
patiently waiting for

She has all the combinations

That comprise to make a unique individual of
select

That image has been tarnished

As a silver teacup, or as a stain-glass window

Smudged...

It has broken the development of trust

I blame not her for these mishaps

She is human as I, and is entitled to mistakes

Nor do I blame myself for becoming entrapped with
the beauty of her

I blame it on the sun

The way that its magnificent rays shined upon her

I blame it on the moon

The way that its dark night had not shown her
darkness

But most of all

I blame it on the stars

Because none of them shined as bright as her

Until the asteroid came

Then crushed what I thought was solid

Which prints inside my membrane

Sadness and Joy

Nothing is truly unbreakable

My mind tells me not to blame him either

For he did what I had done

When I entered the atmosphere

Deepened the crater someone else had built

Now our love has deteriorated

Leaving the eternal soars within her

And my heart

Differences

What is the difference?

Between me and another man

The difference is...

Differences are different in everyone

Only a small percentage of people see them

People tend to state someone reminds them of
someone

Who is completely opposite of a man?

People also tend to categorize someone in this
category

We were told not judge a book by its cover

Instead, people read the first page

Then close the novel completely

All books look the same after that

Visions

All I see are gray clouds

No stars

No grass

No sun

I guess it is true then

The sun never shines in the ghetto

All I see are gray clouds

No moon

No rainbows

No blue sky

I guess it is true then

It only rains in the ghetto

Now when I look up

All I see are gray clouds

Where is the good, where is the love?

All I see is blight

How can we grow with no light?

It only rains here!

But look off into the far distance

A small tree grows amongst the weeds

Maybe I was wrong then

Everything does not need the sun to grow

All I see is hope now

Keep Moving

You should never stop walking

I am always on a constant move

I keep my eyes open

My head up

As I look to the left

I see dust

As I look to the right

I see the same

The road is a long empty one

They are no other travelers on my road

Only intersections of mine and theirs

We acknowledge one another and keep moving

At times it may get lonely

However, the motivation of my destination keeps
me moving

My shoes are demolished

All I Got

All I got is myself in the physical form

Born into an unjust society

Surrounded by envy

The love that is given is unseen

Sometimes I wonder

What is my purpose?

What was I placed here for?

I feel no love

I feel only hatred

I am enraged inside of Hell's grasp

All I got is myself in this physical form

No matter how bad I feel

I am truly blessed, and I never forget that

I am thankful for where I am

Maybe it is human instinct to want more

When in fact, I have more than what I deserve

Spoiled

How can I be so selfish?

With all I got in this physical form

On My Road

My shirt is torn

My pride is strong

I cannot see forward on this path

The dim light and fog are strong

I could not tell you what is behind me

Not because I do not want to, but because I never
looked back

I just keep trotting on

My road to success

Smiles and Tears

3

Walk with Me

Walk with me

Experience what I experience

Through all the ups

Through all the lows

It is a steady pace at a calm rate

Trying to build solid ground in space

See my mistakes I make

The tactics I use to correct them

Look at my pain

Look at my frustration

From not having joy or happiness

So, walk with me

Experience what I do daily, but do not forget

Everything that we do

Is a learning experience

Come Home with Me

Come home with me

Welcome to my world

The world I was born into

I was not made for this life

No one was made for this life

We were molded into it

What are your options when you have none?

A death is what saved my life

Now I understand the reason behind things

Others tend to forget

That is why I remind them

So, if you have never seen the struggle

Come home with me

Look around...

Tell me what you do not see

Opportunity is the word

How many will look for it?

Not many

This is home to me

The Ugly World

The sky is a sight

The hills are beautiful

The mountains are gorgeous

The ocean is smooth

The sequoia is calm

With so much beauty around us

Why is the world so ugly?

Take a look around
And tell me what you...
or better yet tell me what you don't see
oppurtunity is the word
yes, there's a way out of every situation
But how many urban youths will look for it as long as I
Not many is the answer
This is hope to me

The sky blue sky is a wonderful site
The rolling hills are a beautiful scene to notice
The rocky and mishaped mountains are good to cross
The aquatic ocean is a great place to swim
under the leaves of a giant oak is a relaxing place to sit
All of these things and more describe nature
But with all of these aspects of life
I ask the simple question
with so much beauty in and around us
why is the world unified so ugly

As I calmly sit
Sit here and reminist my past
I'm ashamed to say that what I've seen
Is the way things were meant for
even if Life is full of so much anguish and heart
Not just in my environment But all of them
Its the same story everywhere
Just sung to a different melocolony tune
If you listen carefully you may hear the guitar
strings being struck by the musicians fingers
We all have our notes in the songs being played
Some are in unison some may be solo

Patience

As I sit and reminisce my past
I am not ashamed to say what I have seen
This is the way things are
Was all of this meant for?
Even if it was...
Life is full of anguish and hurt
It is the same story everywhere
Sung to a different melancholy tune
If you listen carefully
You may hear the guitar string
It is being struck by the musicians' fingers
We all have our notes in the songs being played
Some songs are in unison
Some may be solo
However, they are all played
I will be ready
When it is my time to be heard

21

If you were a deck of cards

You would be the queen of hearts

You have taken mine

If this was a chess set

I would be your pawn and follow your moves

In this game of love

Your affection is a song

Being played within my soul

What makes you so special?

If you ask me...

I would not know where to begin

You have so many distinct attributes

But my favorite is what you have stolen from me

The heart

Dreams

The other night as I closed my eyes to dream
Tears fell from my eyes
I see the curiosity in your eye
You ask why?
I had a nightmare
You and I no longer existed
I am nothing without you girl
A fire without the flame
I know nothing without you
I can hardly maintain
Me with no you
Is the earth with no sea
A sky with no clouds
A bird with no wings
As you can see, I have nothing
You are my everything
I need you to help me make it through
You are and always will be in my heart
Simply put
That is the way my life would be
Without you

A Cool Breeze

A cool breeze of Winter is on the way

It will soon end Fall's day

Before that, Summer heated up plans

Spring sprung up, faster than expected

The Four Seasons are more than weather

It is a part of me

My Winter being tranquil

My Spring being energetic

My Summer being joyous

My Fall being quiet

Circling myself as I revolve

Pondering thoughts as I evolve

Influencing my moods and actions

Cold as Winter's night

Fickle as Spring's weather

Hot as Summer's day

Level as Fall's heart

All being who I am as a person

Maybe we all have our seasons inside

Thank You

At this moment in time

I would like to have permission

To thank all my artificial friends

All my unloving family members

I would like to thank them all for turning their
backs on me

In the end, it made me stronger

In the end, it made me a better man

A better individual

As a result of them wishing for failure

It made me push harder to succeed

Today, as a young man I have survived an unjust
society

It makes my life a nectar

Rich and sweet

Phoenix

There I was standing on the corner

Opposite to where it all began

The temperature

Hot and humid

The same as my attitude

To my left I notice a group of rats

Eating the long-forgotten trash in the street

A piece of wood then suddenly falls to the ground

Just as so many other pieces of wood had fell
before it

Just as what had stood there previously

All my memories just like the house burned to the
ground

Never to rise or be seen again

Who Am I?

Who am I?
What is my purpose?
What am I to accomplish?
Am I the same as everyman?
Or am I a unique breed of something?
Am I the starring actor in my life?
Or could I be a supporting cast in yours?
Everyone has a story, and mines has yet to be told
Listened to and understood
I am a young man in a subpar world
Surrounded by more negativity than good
Looking for my true calling in life
I am not completely confused
Truth be told I know what is meant for me
The problem is
At times, I just do not think I am ready

Broken Dreams

4

Crossfire

In the middle of crossfire

I have deepened the wound implanted in me

To the dismay of others, I show no visible signs of
harm

I am accustomed to this, and wounds heal fast

On one side of me is the land I have dreamed of

On the other side is a place where nightmares
come from

I consider myself a fair person

Inside though, it is as if Lucifer holds me in his
arms

I am in reach of what I indeed want

But every time I reach...

The carpet beneath me is pulled opposite to the
direction headed

Causing mass friction in my life

There I am in the sight of two worlds

One is good...

The other needs not to be spoken on

The gravity of them both pulling me

Back and forth as an eternal war

Time is running out

If I do not reach my destination

I will be trapped in the middle of space

Stars

Stars are brightest at night they say...

I disagree

Stars are brightest in the day

If it takes darkness to view beauty

You cannot truly see

If you can spot stars in the light

You see beauty when all things are visible

The night is a place of mystery

It is then when most eyes are opened

After the sun is set

The day has ended

Chapters of many novels have closed

Not everyone is given the eyesight to see

Have you noticed stars in the day?

Or

Are you blind to the beauty that a closer star covers?

Nearing the Future

Here I am staring...

Staring into the future

Not looking back at the past

It is too painful at times

The reminder of what has taken place

Hurts me even more than what occurred

When I was previously hurt

Whenever my mind comes to a blank slate

No longer do I wish to look at what is in the past

Nor even the present

But only the future

I have become nearsighted

Poem 45

I have not a thing to lose
For my mind is anorexic
So I have all to gain
For it will soon be obese
As I steadily feed it with nutrients
That I have consumed from life lessons
The game never ends in my sight
There is no such thing as a loss
Valuable lessons are learned with each careful movement
Watching others succeed
Just motivates me for what is soon to come
Come into my sight and stay
As it has in so many others
I will make it
I know now of no failure
If I've failed at anything, it was
Not doing what so many expected me to do
Lose

Poem 46

Stop It Now
'Okay
Not Yet
Are You Sure
Of Course I Am
I completely understand
I knew You Would
So
What is It
Nothing
I was wondering
What
Its Not Important

Nothing to Lose

I have not a thing to lose

My mind is anorexic

I have all to gain

It will soon be obese

I feed it with nutrients consumed from life lessons

The game never ends in my sight, there is no such
thing as a loss

Valuable lessons are learned with each careful
movement

Watching others succeed motivates me

It will come into my sight and stay

I will make it

I know of no failure

If I have failed at anything

It was at not doing what so many expected me to
do

Lose

Grabbing My Thoughts

As I was thinking today

A thought sprung up in my head

It brought qualities of new

Excitement

Anticipation

Then questions

Which made me ponder much longer

Had I mistakenly skipped over this?

Had I been so blind I could not understand

Had I not seen what was meant for me

Or could it all have been a figment of imagination?

A dream of some sort

How could something so realistic be so unreal?

It is all within arm's reach, but do I really want to
grasp it?

If so, what am I waiting for?

We all have dreams and success starts in your
head

Which is where dreams are born

It is up to us if we make them real

Then continue to feed them to keep them breathing

Grab those dreams

Before they pull away

You Are My Heaven

What is heaven to you?

I know what it is to me

But I cannot imagine what it would be like without
you

Trees of honey

Rivers of milk

Rainbows of love

Would not be gratifying

If you were not there to spend it with me

I am the moon

You are my earth

I revolve around you faithfully

The smile of your face is my nourishment

It feeds me to please you

Touched in my heart by your care

It has given me happiness

I thank you for that genuinely

If it was possible

I would stay longer for you

Heaven can wait.

Numb

I only have a few things that I care for

I could never figure out why

But as I aged I saw things more clearly

It appeared as if

I was some sort of an emotionless being

That is not true

The things that I cherish are truly everything to me

Without those few individuals and things, I am cold

That is what keeps me breathing and warm inside

Maybe that is why so few understand me

My personality, my being, even my intellect

It often goes underappreciated just as clouds in the sky

It is not until the rain comes when people feel the mist

Not knowing what they are amid

All that I have is loved because there is nothing else

So, I have learned to appreciate it

With all this knowledge I have gained

I am still numb at times

Because other than that

I feel I have no feelings

It is Going to Get Hard

It is going to get hard kid

You still must live through it

What have you to lose?

Nothing...

What have you to gain?

Everything

So, it should be an easy solution

Many go off track

Wandering far off the designated path

Some take the slow and steady route

Just as the sloth

Taking it one step at a time

Carefully recognizing past mistakes

Which are you?

Can you hear the roaring of the sea?

Or

Do you not listen to the truth?

Treat your ears like your eyes

Keep them very wide open

If you were to miss it (Opportunity)

Do not hover over the past

Just as I lived my life

I will let you live yours

Pains of Love

5

The Odd House

In the center of the block

Sits an odd house

It is the pearl of the neighborhood

Other homes are larger and more expensive

It is something about the old house that draws
attention

Some say it just does not belong here

Others say it fits right in

Many of the homes are similar

This one is not

People argue that they hate its differences

Many still do

Others have opened their doors to change

In my opinion

It brings color to the environment

That is filled with so much of the same

Butterflies

T he butterflies are

Natural

Organic

Peaceful

Remaining calm in the ever-harsh environment of
nature

Carefully gliding through the warm air

Surrounded by peace and tranquility

The ever-present noises of nature playing their
tune

As they grow and mature

The sun beams on their perfectly crafted wings

Creating such designs as eyes and ears

The natural, naturalistic look

Is pleasing to the eye

Just as anything else earthly

It is a shame they forget about the butterfly

When You Have Something Good

When you have something good...

You better hold on to it

Cause you never know if you will ever have it again

Something so nice you cannot help but to miss

You may wonder why it went wrong and how it began

That question will be simply answered

Yet never easily understood

Never truly accepted

Never really reasoned why

Not every bird can fly

We must never talk of the next day

Until we see the sunrise

Poem 59

When you have something good
you better hold on to it
Cause you never know if you'll ever have it again
Something so nice you can help but to Miss
You may wonder why it went wrong and now it began
That question will be simply answered
and ever so easily understood
Never truly accepted and never reasoned why
Not every bird can fly
We must never tell of the next day
until we see the sunrise

Poem 60

Am I my brothers keeper?
The guardian of his soul
The shoulder to lean on the person to console
The one to correct his rights
And white out his mistakes made
The one to correct the wrinkle creases in his used
Should I put my visible dreams aside
So that I may help him find his guided path
As a child I was his everything
And sadly All that he had
We were a unite seperated by none
But as we matured the evidence spring
The relationship was not that of origin

Brother's Keeper

Am I my brother's keeper?

The guardian of his soul

His shoulder to lean on

His person to console

Should I put my dreams aside?

So I may help him find his guided path

I blame his problems upon myself

All too many nights my eyes have leaked dry tears

All for naught is what my brain said

What a terrible thought is what my heart spoke

I can only push so much

Someone who has not learned to walk

Speak for so much

For someone who has chosen not to talk

Life is about options

I opted for a better route

I keep him in my heart

But I follow my brain

The Road to Freedom

My road towards freedom was not an easy one

The trials and tribulations I have seen are harsh...

Rough and rugged as the tough side of the
mountain

There is no problem anyone cannot mount

If faith is present in the heart

Learning Experiences

You learn something new everyday

Every day I am constantly learning

Learning something that may affect my future

Whatever it may hold for me

Inside of its hands

Handling me with care

Or maybe even carelessness

Depending on what happens in my story

I learned that as a young boy

It has been here ever since

Constant

Not moving a step as if its

Paralyzed

Stationed

In my brain like easy lessons learned in maturing

Stuck with it

Feeling as if the consequence of it

Is as positive as the flower

I have embraced it, and accepted it

It will not be taken for granted

As so much other stuff is taken for granted by me

The Broken Clock

In the middle of the living room

Sits a robust and aged grand medieval clock

It is gold around the borders

Its hands are made of the finest steel

Over time it has become difficult to see

Many never see its beauty

The clock has read the same time long as I
remember

No one tries to fix it, and see what the problem is

Neither do they look up to read the time

Surprisingly...

The large clock still ticks with every passing
second

The kids consider this annoying and a waste of
space

Only if they knew

Even a broken clock is right two times a day!

Same

Changed?

Who me?

Never that

I am the same

I never forgot where I came from or what I did to
get from that

I am as humble as a singer's voice

Shhhhhhhh...You hear that sound?

That is the voices of these streets

That is the voice of me...

If it was not for that tune

I may not be

Since We Last Spoke

It has been a while since we last spoke

Do not be mad

What was I supposed to do?

Me without you

Was no hard question

At times, my ability I questioned

What would you do?

Answer that question

Call me whatever you may feel

I deservingly deserve your mistreatment

I used you daily, and screamed hate on you

Secretly, I was falling hard for you

Harder than what I was supposed to

I hid you from the world

Hurt you, AND I unknowingly

My everything is you

You need to be let out of my pages, and into others
across the world

No longer do I care what others think

I love what you have made me

You have both inked my heart, and my book

My blood now pumps love, and it feeds my soul
with your magic

Apologetic Thoughts

I am not the apologetic type

For I am far from that

Just was not raised that way

Taught not to behave that way

So it hurts even more for what I have to say

I was told to learn from your mistakes

But expressing them was unnecessary

Some things I have done have been that also

I know that you notice that

I know you hear of my scandalous acts

They say things about me I did not do

At the same time though

Some if not more are true

Karma always comes around

It is just the way things work

I have been honest the whole time

Maybe we can construct, build, and make it work

Maybe we do not need it (each other)

The cards are in your hands

You determine my next move

In so many words, I have told you what I came to say

What I just cannot say (I am sorry)

Songs of Sorrow

6

When I Close My Eyes

When I close my eyes at night

Only I know the pain

Explaining it is meaningless

You can see it in my eyes

For I know I have sinned

That is why I pray daily

Walk with my head up

Look up towards the heavens

Then humbly cry for help

It is what I need

It is not what I want

Throughout all the hurt I have endured

I am blessed to be where I am

Basic human nature is in me

I hate it

The greed and the want for more

I desire it

The things I have done to obtain it

Knowing that I am blessed

The evil inside me still wants it

Pray for me

Pray with me

Pray that it works for the better

Coming to My Senses

Of the five senses

It is sight that truly intrigues me

I observe the good and the bad in people

I learned who is trustworthy and who is not

Learned more than what I ever thought

All of this with vision

I evaluate every situation I can, and everyone I
have met

There lays one problem with this

How can I see what I cannot look at?

Myself

As I gaze into the mirror

What I see confuses me

What I see is a good person

What does the world see?

Do they notice the cut in my brows?

The slight unevenness of my eyes

Do they see just another person?

I only see my faults when I look at myself

That is why I touch my face to feel them

I am not conceited

I am only concerned

I want to feel what they see

Sky Is the Limit

The things that I care for are limited

The love I have for those have a limit

It is the sky

Watch me raise my hands

Watch me reach up

Gratitude

Thank you

For all that you have done...

Done for me and my siblings

It was not much at times

But it was always much more than what you were able to do

I appreciate that more than what I may ever express to you

That is why I have placed my feelings on this page for you

Hopefully, you can understand it

I have been through some rough times

You were there holding my hand, one day you will not be there

The hurt I will feel I cannot imagine, nor do I want to

I have embraced the fact, that things will change

One thing that will never change is

The love that I have for you

Walk to My Tune

Take a walk with me

A stroll through all my mishaps

And the negatives of everyday life

Maybe you can relate to many of the tribulations
and trials

Maybe you will not be able to

Whatever it may or may not be

Just know the words to my song

If you cannot hear me sing it

Lost Again

Here I am again

Lost

Found in an unreasonable position

My past decisions have costed me greatly

Affected me to the point it hurts

Burning inside wildly as a wildfire

Directionless

As if encompassing all points of the compass

Motionless

Just as the tranquil waves of the arctic

Undisturbed

Patiently waiting for the right moment

The moment in which all questions will be
answered

No doubt will rest

My time is almost here

Hold Your Head

Keep your head up my child

Stay calm, stay strong my child

This is the eye of the storm

You have realized what is to come

You have been patient too long

Your time is coming shortly

After the last drop falls

Sunny days are appreciated after rain

Pain has run his course

The hour is now for the bluer sky

The second is now for the greener hills

The moment is now yours

Remain Constant

Every so often

My heart goes numb

I feel as if I have no feelings

As if my body is composed of sheet rock and metal

Cold

No warmth whatsoever lies within

Nothing outside of it is felt

It has been this way too long

I cannot let my guard down, and become wounded

It hurts

So, I shall remain constant

Stay Strong

I am a strong soul

Been like this since I can remember

Guess it comes from my mother

It must run in my family also

You must be like this in my bloodline

Good times are seen on television, and are
dreamed of here

Nevertheless, all that I have is cherished

Appreciated

Loved

Cared for dearly

It is hard

I stay strong regardless

I have no other option

What...

Never Look directly at Sun
Its rays May be its Magnificent to gaze at
Its light may be to bright to question
To strong to Imagine
But still lingers the question
Why not
Sure we've all heard the rumors, myths, and lies
But do you know anyone who's successfully tried
Stared with all of their might in their eyes
Until the squenched closed and tears sheltered down
What did you Say
Are you Serious with the words you Speak
Me
Nah I'll pass on that one
Only Fools look directly at the Sun

They always ask me
Why am I always laughing
Simple
Sometimes things are just funny to me
Its funny to see
The unfairness and unjust that occurs around me
To keep myself composed
I took up this remedy
I pray every what ends rage

Only A Fool

W hat...

Never look directly at the sun

Its rays may be magnificent to gaze at

Its light may be too bright to question

Too strong to imagine

Still lingers the question

Why not?

We have all heard the rumors, myths, and lies

But do you know anyone who has successfully
tried?

Stared with all their might with their eyes

Until they squinch closed and tears sheltered down

What did you say?

Are you serious with the words you speak?

Me!

Nah, I will pass on that one

Only fools look directly at the sun

No Laughing Matter

They always ask me

Why am I always laughing?

Simply put...

Sometimes things are just funny to me

It is funny to see

The unfairness and unjust that occurs around me

To keep myself composed

I took up this remedy

I pray over what endows rage

That is what I call power

Bless my enemies, I hold no grudges

Many are unneeded

Misunderstood, overcomplicated, its leads to no good

I have come to learn that

So now when something crazy happens

I give a smirk, smile, and laugh

It is funny to me

When I See You

I see you walking everyday

Not once did I approach you, or ask your name

Introduce myself, or even glance too long

Not because I do not want to

Inside, I burn dearly to do so

But see, my opinion of you has already been
formatted

Your personality is already described

Maybe you have noticed me before also

If not

There is a first time for everything

I am willing to change that

That is, if you are open to the fact

My first real words to you have been replayed,
countless times

The words in return you will say vary

Depending on your mood

Maybe even a significant other

Honestly, that is not why I have not talked to you

The real reason is, I do not know you

I have imagined what you are like

How smart you are, and how ambitious also

I have placed you on the highest pedestal available

There you are standing tall

When I See You

I am afraid that once I speak
All of that will be erased
Things are never what they seem
This way you will not mess things up for me
And I will cherish the moment of not knowing
Until I am ready to come down
Facing realization that, you are no different
Then anyone else

A Big Misunderstanding

To understand me...

Is to understand the wind

The way it breezes pass

The way it cools one's soul

The way it settles one's mind

To understand me...

Is to understand the seas

The way the waves roll

The way the waves push

The way the waves relax

To understand me...

One must understand

The way it is

The way it feels

The way it hurts

Sure, there is a way to understand pain

But who understands here on earth?

Clouded Skies

7

Look Up

Anytime I am feeling down

There is only one place to look

Up

When one has fallen to the pits

There is only one place to look

Up

Down and out

Placed in a situation where no choice is left

Left with the only option

The option to bow

There is no other answer

He is the only choice (Yahweh)

We must pick it

Right Back Where I Started

Here I am, right back...

Right back, like I never left

Like I have been before

Because I have, before all of this changed

There are always two sides of each door

Which side are you on?

The inside?

Or are you on the outside, looking into the house?

I am the prodigal product

But I have held the quotient

I have divided many things

My remainder remains

Lingering under the bar

I must quickly substitute things

Because my problem may be the next solved

What People Say

Some say that I am corrupted

I beg to differ with that

It is the things inside of me, and the ways to obtain

The thing that makes them go wild

Whatever it is that places on their face a smile

It could be anything

Varying for different people

In quite different situations

As I rotate my shoulders away from them

Ending the daylight that they see

It is obvious to see

The bad that is present inside of me

I am held in their hands

Filled in their heads

It is the greed of love that feeds them

It is the greed of love that kills them

But they cry and tell me I am wrong

Have I polluted myself?

Cut my own hair?

Drunken my own wines?

No, I have not

It is you that has done this

It is your fault

looking into the house
I'm the prodicals product
But I held the quotient
And have divided many things
My remainder remains
lingering under the bar
I must quickly substitute thing
For My problem may be the next completed

The last time we spoke
Things didn't turn out as planned
Or even went the initial way I had hope
I had my few choice of words
All we all know you had more than your share
I didn't make a mistake
Because I knew what I was doing
So I won't dare say that
Excuses are unreal, and told to make the sun show
Shew through the sky on a cloudy day
Do I want to get back together
Of course I would love
But maybe this is the best decision now
The future
Who knows what her hands may hold
It could be me and you
Or

Last Time We Spoke

The last time we spoke

Things did not turn out as planned

I had my few choices of words

And we all know

You had more than your share

I did not make a mistake

Because I knew what I was doing

So, I will not dare say that

Excuses are unreal, and told to make the sun
show...

Show through the skies on a cloudy day

Do I want to get back together?

Of course

I would love to hold you, but maybe this is the best
decision now

The future

Who knows what her hands may hold?

It could be me and you

Share

Share what makes you happy

Share what makes you smile

Share what gets you excited

Just for a little while

Tell me what gives you troubles

Tell me what gives you stress

Tell me what gives you sorrow

That puts your kindness to test

Why do you laugh during the day?

Why do you cry during the night?

Why do you hide your feelings?

When we can see them in plain sight

Finally

F inally, I have found

What I have been looking to find

I have discovered I am lost

Forgotten

Left

Misplaced

At least that is how it feels, to be caught up in
these winds

Being spun around in that circular motion

In every thinkable direction

Directionless

Hoping to find direction itself

Wherever it may be

Wherever it is

However, I cannot reach it

No matter how far my outreached hand extends

No matter how long my broken heart beats with
faith

It is still not clear

I pray it finds me

by I've Found
I've been finding looking to find
Discovered I'm Lost

Torn, Left, Misplaced Wrongfully
At least that is how It feels
Feels to be caught up in these winds
Being spun around in that circular motion
  In every thinthimic direction
            directionless
  Hoping to find direction itself
    Where ever it may be
    Where ever it is
    However thought I cannot reach it
      No matter how far my outreached hand.
                              Extending
      No matter how long my squenched eyes see
      No matter how long my broken hearts beats with faith
        · It still isn't clear
  I can only pray it finds me

I'm infatuated with your character
and the intelligence your brain is always god of
I must honestly admit
I've not once encountered anyone similiar
    Similiar to the true things you possess
    and If I did
  I probably wouldn't be able to recognize them
    For the reason that you would be being thoughtful
    An something of your stature should be

The way things work is strange
At the sunset of the day it seems
Seems as if things went as planned / No Matter the predicament
The intended outcome of things is hare to visualize
  Just as the ending of this poem is
  What do you think will happen
    Sometimes thoughts can be hurtful
    Only if you allow it
  Many may not understand me
    But those that don't aren't thinkers
      They just think

My Infatuation for You

I am infatuated with your character

The intelligence your brain is comprised of

I must honestly admit

I have not once encountered anyone that has the
things you possess

If I did...

I probably would not be able to recognize them

Because you would be being thought of

As something of your stature should be

The Way Things Work

The way things work is strange

At the sunset of the day, it seems as if things went
as planned

No matter the predicament

The intended outcome is to visualize

Just as the ending of this poem is

What do you think will happen?

Sometimes thoughts can be hurtful

If you allow them to be

Many may not understand me

But to those that do not

They are not thinkers

They just think

We Have Been Here Before

There you are

Looking at me as if I do not know

I will not lie and say I am prepared for you

I am not sure what you are capable of

I do know you will not take me alive

I have a shield on my side

You may play with my mind

You may play with my brain

My heart belongs to Yahweh, just as my soul

You may break me down (Evil)

You may step on my fingers

Every time you break this puzzle

He puts me back together with more pieces

The picture is getting clearer

I see the sky

I see jealousy in your eyes

You have made a hobby of assaulting me

I fight back

Swinging with all my might

Running with all my strength

Headed for the gates

Lord save me

I am Not Ready

It could be different

But right now, this is how it should be

There is no one else...

Nobody who can feel the void I am about to create

Seeing you hurt

Is more than what I can bare

I am not ready yet...

No matter what you tell me

I know you are not either

So, do not lie to me

If it is truly meant...

We will find each other again, and the outcome will
be reassuring

If not...

It was fun while it lasted

Blind Love

If love is not blind

Why do I feel this way?

Why do I see us together?

Why do I only see your good?

Why do you not feel the same?

Is it something I said?

Something I did?

The love I have for you is like none other

I refuse to see what everyone tells me

I just want to win your love back

I am tired of losing all that I care for

I have tried to hold us together

I could not see your hearts movement

Love is blind

So, I may never see why

The wind is still blowing
The fire is burning
The water is running
The sun is shining
The clouds are moving
And the days are passing
And so is the time
The time has come
It is now time for me to mature
Me to grow into the man
The man my Mother wanted me to be
To live the way she would want
No longer can I watch time pass w/o change
Change in my characteristics
Change is good for the soul
At least that is what I was told
Then how come the more I do good
The less it is appreciated
And I still feel the wind
I guess some things don't change

What's going on old man
What you've been up to?
Years tough sounds good
Glad to hear you've been doing well
I've been Okay Myself Things are getting

Still Is

The wind is still blowing

The fire is still burning

The water is still running

The sun is still shining

The clouds are still moving

The days are still passing

So is the time

The time has come

It is now time for me to mature

Me to grow into the man my mother wants me to
be

To live the way, she wants

No longer can I watch time move without change...

Change in my characteristics

Change is good for the soul

At least that is what I was told

How come the more I do, the less it is appreciated?

I still feel the wind

I guess some things do not change

Cartoons and Reality

I always did watch cartoons; it was a way of life
growing up

All the other kids did as well

As I aged it seemed like they disappeared

Where did all the cartoons go?

The older I got, the less I saw

I miss the animated characters, now I see things
similar in my life

All the unrealistic things are gone

It is as if the cartoons went away just as I aged,
now it is all real

Giving me no imagination of a better situation

This is the real world, nothing is animated here

No waking up from a dream

No changing the channels

This is what you get

Seek, Find, Share

Red, blue, and yellow
The three primary colors
The beginning of every known...
Known color of the prism that is
Together creating all sorts of beauty
Cherished by the eye
Underappreciated by the person
Stared at by the pupil...
Pupil I am
A student of things I have seen
A philosopher of countless encounters
A physician of physical sciences
A teacher of knowledge I have learned
Still, I remain humble as a bee
Thoughtful as the brain
Sharing all I know

93

Time changes, just as the day passes
The Moon rises
Just as the sun sets
Why
Why is that you ask
Of course you could take the science approach
But what does that really answer
Nothing
It just tells you how things work
Not why
which leaves the question mark undotted
unfinished as the artists stroke
seemingly left untouched like the painted picture
had run empty
empty of inn
Which leaves all too many people lost
And here is where faith enters
Without it you are just the same as a stray
Searching for a home you may never find

we All Need help
There's No secret about it
Let us help our brothers, sisters and friends here
And here we'll be
waving and cheering
As They walk their ways home

94

Breaking Old Habits is so hard to do
Oh how so true
Knowing right from wrong is easy
But staying on the right truth is easier said then done
Coming from where I'm from
The Negativity in the air has a freshness
The fresh scent of wrong
Being accepted with no questions after
Not to get things mixed up but
I'm not exactly a rose
But neither Am I the prick that sticks
Cuts and Aches between the creaks of the skin
The middle of the road is where you may spot me
Restless
Still Asking why
Its so hard to leave bad habits behind

Time

Time changes
Just as the day passes
Just as the moon rises
Just as the sun sets
It is the way things work
Question marks are undotted
Unfinished as the artist's stroke
Empty of ink
Empty of life
Empty of thought
Void of time

Old Habits

Breaking old habits is hard to do

Oh, how so true

Knowing right from wrong is easy

But staying on the right track is easier said than done

Coming from where I am from

The negativity in the air has a freshness

The fresh scent of wrong

Being accepted with no questions after

Not to get things mixed up, but I am not exactly a rose

Neither am I the prick that sticks,

Neither the cut that aches between the cracks of the skin

The middle of the road is where you may spot me

Restless, still asking why

It is so hard to leave bad habits behind

The Devil on My Back

The devil is on my back

Try to understand how I feel inside

The poverty provides fires

It keeps me burning inside

Lord, please forgive me for my sins

For I know the consequences of what I did

No longer do I want to live how I had lived

Too many nights I prayed for things to be right

I still fight the urge

Too many times I am weakened again

I know what is wrong

I know what is right

The hand I was dealt left-ed me

Which will never be right

December 13th

8

As the Day Passes

As the day passes

I get more and more restless

I can no longer remain patient

My nerves are jumping as if I am hooked

I do want it badly, but I cannot handle it now

Nor can anyone else handle it

But it is me, I cannot hide that fact

How would it look for me to turn my back?

Look away as if I cannot see the shadow left in the dark

It will follow me around

Haunting and hawking my every move

As if it is ashamed of what I plan to do

Why me?

I ask for your prayers, I need them

I want the prayers badly, and they do not

My decision cannot be overturned

Its turns out

I am lost, and I do not want to be forgotten

So here they are
 My last words of this chapter
 Not only of this Book
 But of this chapter in my life
  Change is going on around me
  But it doesn't happen to me
You See, I call it the maturing-factor
  Factored in with me learning more
  More About Myself, friends, and lifestyle
  It was never easy
  And It certainly was and never will be fair
  But This life that was shown To me
  Only when I was a blind adolescent
  In search of a True happiness that only he can help me
   And I will find It One day
   I don't know when, where, or how it will happen realize
    But It will occur
   Because I have faith Stored inside of me
   Trapping it as the spider does its prey
    I feed off of it
  I Thank you All
 Espiecially All of My Friend that turned their backs on to
   It Made Me Stronger
    Smile Bigger
    Listen Harder
    See Clearer
    Think Bolder
   And I+ Molded me to the Man you See person
    Me

Poem 100

So here they are

My last words of this chapter

Not only of this book, but of this chapter in life

Change is going on around me

I call it evolution

Factored in with me learning more about myself

It was never easy

It will never be fair

This life is what was shown to me

I was a blind adolescent

In search of a true happiness to be realized

I do not know when, where, or how it will happen...

But it will occur

I have faith stored inside of me

Trapping it as the spider does it prey

I feed off it...

It made me stronger

Smile bigger

Listen harder

See clearer

Think bolder

It has molded me into the person you see

Me

My Dawning of Time

My time has arisen

I have been in the silhouettes far too long

I see the stage clearly

I must step into the limelight

It is my shining time

The cameras are on

The lights are flashing

Disappoint, I will not

I have worked too hard to get to this point

The place where you see me now

Was a brutal place to make it

A journey of dangers, and unexpected slips

Falter, I did not

Did I continue?

Yes, I did

Now I see a place full of mystery

What it holds is unknown

One thing I do know is

It is time for me to find out

And I will

My Hurt

Seeing that I am hurt

Should hurt you more

I am aching in pain

It is overbearing on my heart

Not a beat goes by without it pumping for you

All of this does no good

Why are you pushing me away?

What did I do to deserve this?

My love is stunned

Why are you so unnerved...?

Talk to me...

Express your feelings...

Otherwise, I will be in the same position

Unaware

Naive

Oblivious

Let us not take that route

What is going on?

Just Tell Me Why

Why do you do?

What you do?

You do it for some concealed reason

You have made a pastime of striking me

I struggle back fighting

Always moving with all my strength

Sprinting for the gates

Please spare me

Mistakes

Never have I made such a mistake

As I did when I let you go

I pushed you into them

As I pulled myself away from you

How could I be so foolish?

How could I not let you know?

The way I was feeling

The way I was hurting

The way I was thinking

As I glance into my future

It is now void of your presence

It is filled with emptiness inside of my heart

Pain inside of my body

But your love is still inside of my veins

Word spreads fast and wounds heal slow

Should I lie and wish for your happiness?

Should I smile and say that I am happy?

Should I be honest and tell the truth?

I am afraid to move on because I still love you

Even though I am selfish

Even though I am wrong

These are the words to my tune

These are the notes to our song

I placed myself here
So I will not complain of unfairness
I had a fair chance to leave
But I willingly walked back
back into the place I swore not to
Here Are the results
The lights dim and so is the outlook
Ib I come up out of this
My heart cries for change
My brain speaks that is nonsense
non-existent in the place I am
   Inside of a whirlwind imaginable
Of Almost every element of negatives
The positive being I see that
And That's about where it stays

When the cold chilly wind of winter hits my face
It hits me —
Just how cool the world actually is
windchill added
The Breezing breezes of carelessness
have carried me to the brink
Almost to the edge of wondering
Where did Summer go
Is she ever returning
Or am I destined to remain here forever
Fall passed just as quick as he appeared
Spring, sprung up and then proceeded to fade
So winter with all of his mishaps have come
got comfortable, and refuses to remove himself
Was it always this cold
Or did I just always wear a jacket before

I Am to Blame

I placed myself here

So I will not complain of unfairness

I had a fair chance to leave

I willingly walked back

Back into the place I swore not to go

Here are the results

The lights are dim

So is the outcome

I pray to come up out of this

My heart cries for change

My brain speaks that it is nonsense

Non-existent in the place where I am

Inside of a whirlwind

Of almost every imaginable element of negatives

The positive being, I see that (whirlwind)

That is about where it stops

December 13th

When the cold wind of winter hits my face

It hits me just how cold the world is...

The windchill has been added

Freezing breezes of carelessness

Have carried me to the brink of the edge wondering

Where did summer go?

Will she will ever return?

Am I destined to remain here forever?

Fall passed just as quick as she appeared

Spring sprung up, and then proceeded to fade

Winter with all her mishaps have come

She is comfortable and refuses to remove herself

Was it always this cold...?

Or did I just always wear a jacket before...?

;

www.ingramcontent.com/pod-product-compliance
Lightning Source LLC
Chambersburg PA
CBHW031626040426
42452CB00007B/700